Helen Kendrick

A decade of working in the architecture and heritage world in Glasgow has led Helen into some of the city's most interesting historic interiors, both public and private. Helen is a regular contributor to the media on issues regarding Glasgow's heritage and has curated exhibitions on subjects including the Glasgow Style and Victorian architecture. She is Glasgow's representative for the international committee the Reseau Art Nouveau Network, dedicated to promoting Art Nouveau heritage across the world. In her spare time, she likes walking around the city, staring at people's interiors through their windows.

Neale Smith

Neale has been working as a freelance photographer in Glasgow for more than eight years. Following a spell at the Glasgow School of Art and influenced by a love of urban landscapes (and also his father's career as an architect), he has developed a specialism in architectural and interior photography. He has a varied and loyal customer base throughout the built environment, design and infrastructure sectors.

Glasgow Interiors

Helen Kendrick

Photography by Neale Smith

BIRLINN

First published in 2014 by
Birlinn Limited
West Newington House
10 Newington Road
Edinburgh
EH9 1QS

www.birlinn.co.uk

ISBN: 978 1 78027 243 6

British Library Cataloguing-in-
Publication Data

A catalogue record for this book is
available from the British Library

Typeset by Mark Blackadder

Printed and bound by Livonia Print, Latvia

Contents

Foreword

Alex Kapranos
lead singer and guitarist, Franz Ferdinand

When you arrive in a city you judge its character instantly. It's the same as when you meet someone for the first time and survey their faces for signs of compassion, humour, temper or life in the lines of their face, the light in their eyes or the way their lips curve as they smile. When I arrived in Glasgow at the age of ten in 1983 it was as if I was introduced to a dark imposing Victorian industrialist clad in a sombre frock coat of black soot. In its architecture, its history and personality seemed awe inspiring and a little intimidating. It was only after years of living with this personality that the complexities and nuances of its nature were revealed – the richness of life, its capacity to adapt and a unique sense of style that evolved from circumstance and the people who live and lived here.

It's when you step through the walls of those black canyons of tenements and Victorian façades into the tiled closes lit by weak sunlight passing through the coloured glass, that the truth of Glasgow's nature becomes apparent. I have to thank Helen for making me consider that nature again, as when you are overly familiar with a character you take it for granted. Now, as I picture Glasgow on the inside, I realise again what a beautiful place it is.

So, flick through these pages and enjoy this glimpse of a city. If you are familiar with their contents, stop to appreciate what you already know. If it is a first introduction for you, I hope it's the beginning of a strong friendship with a warm and fascinating place, as it was for me thirty-one years ago.

'Bruised and battered but not destroyed'

Dedicated to the Glasgow School of Art
and all who've played a part in its history

Introduction

The life of our city is rich in poetic and marvellous subjects. We are enveloped and steeped as though in an atmosphere of the marvellous; but we do not notice it.

Charles Baudelaire

By looking at the facades of urban buildings and exterior cityscapes, we understand something of a city: its wealth, location, purpose, international connections, local materials and vernaculars. But by looking behind the facades, which we often do not have the chance to do, we learn a story about the people of a city: who these buildings were made for, and why. Often we imagine and re-imagine interior spaces over the years; as they change, whether through desire or necessity, they show us what has changed about our city's communities 200 years on and what's still the same, what's universal.

Mies van der Rohe declared 'architecture is the will of an epoch translated into space'. Architecture is contained space, the world of interiors, real and imagined, and this is relevant to the interiors featured here. Their stories tell us about the city of Glasgow at certain moments in time, those who designed it, those who commissioned it, those who enjoyed it.

Included here are buildings ranging from a mid-eighteenth-century manor house to a mid-twentieth-century cinema, via exotic Victorian swimming baths and an art nouveau publisher's office. We see a seventeenth-century steeple incorporated into a former fish market now acting as a thriving East End artists' studio, and a former tobacco merchant's house now an internationally acclaimed gallery that was for a time a telephone exchange. We find a family villa that has been both a maternity hospital and a retirement home before becoming once again a private residence, and a 100-year-old family-run cafe that has always been a cafe (run by the same family) and hopefully always will be. The buildings featured span nearly 200 years and touch on stories of wealth, religion, industry, prostitution, families, communities, art, entertainment, travel and immigration within the city over the past two centuries.

The cast of characters featured via these buildings include many famous names: artists, architects and entrepreneurs from Glasgow's history, including J.J. Burnet, Alexander Thomson, Stephen Adam, Daniel Cottier, George Walton, James Miller, Kate Cranston and rags-to-riches international cast-iron magnate Walter Macfarlane. Through the contemporary usage and recent developments of the interiors, we see a twenty-first-century cast list emerging; prominent artists, architects and designers such as Jim Lambie, Page\Park and Graven Images feature for the part they are currently playing in preserving and reinterpreting our built heritage.

The buildings of the city's most famous architectural son, Charles Rennie Mackintosh, are however purposefully absent from this book. There are numerous excellent books on Mackintosh that fully explore his work in various contexts: holistic designer-architect; furniture; painter and watercolourist; the tearooms; his patrons; his celebrated collaborations. To say his work has had a dramatic effect on the city is an understatement, but here we celebrate the diverse, world-class and so far largely 'secret' interiors of the city. Inevitably, Mackintosh is referenced throughout – in the context of his relationships with other architects, designers, artists and patrons, and through his design legacy.

The majority of the buildings featured here were constructed between 1870 and 1905, during an economic boom in Glasgow that embraced a burst of creative expression in the city, as many architects, artists and designers channelled the 'new art' – Glasgow Style – in their work. Glasgow's middle-class suburbs to the west and south of the centre expanded rapidly at this time, as wealthier citizens sought to escape the overcrowding of the city centre and East End. Those responsible for building these suburbs, populated by a growing bourgeoisie, adopted the Glasgow Style in their designs, particularly throughout interior ornamentation in homes, public offices and leisure spaces. The widespread popularity of the Glasgow Style amongst the burgeoning middle classes is important in the context of local identity. The essential character and allure of a city is not solely defined by its grand public edifices or architectural icons, but often by the local vernacular and of course the citizens, and nowhere is this more true than in Glasgow. As Scottish urban theorist Patrick Geddes has noted, the prevalent design and architectural style in a city relates strongly to the social personality, regional character and 'life force' of its citizens; channelling Glasgow Style ornamentation, with its delicate colour palette and motifs drawn from the nature surrounding the city, and close links with the European avant-garde, was an effective way for the bourgeoisie to identify themselves as modern, civilised and in harmony with the values and taste of the popular artistic scene of the time. Scotland's largest city had developed notoriety throughout the earlier part of the nineteenth century as the 'grim city of the north'; the enthusiastic embracing of the new style in their interiors distanced aspirational citizens from the well-documented notion of Glasgow as a city of grime and immense social problems, including overcrowding, disease and alcoholism.

Glasgow has long been a city with a dual reputation. Known as the Second City of the Empire and the 'Greatest Victorian City in the World', it also had a reputation for poor housing conditions, ill health and poverty. It still has high levels of deprivation and a short life expectancy in some areas, yet it can boast some of the highest numbers of graduates per capita and most expensive houses in Scotland. However, in terms of the preservation of its heritage, the city has, since its successful cultural renaissance, kick-started in 1988 by the Glasgow Garden Festival, become internationally renowned for heritage-led regeneration – finding innovative new uses for redundant buildings and thus enabling them to endure successfully into the future. Almost half of all the buildings in this book now have a new purpose, different from that for which they were originally designed. This unique atmosphere of creativity and innovation in Glasgow is something that has attracted international attention in the twenty-five years since Glasgow's reign as European Capital of Culture in 1990. A prominent part of this innovative quality is undoubtedly due to the Glasgow School of Art's enduring influence on the city. The building itself, the art nouveau masterpiece of Mackintosh and one of the icons of British architecture and interior design, not only influences its own students but has a sequential effect on the entire city, also attracting people from all over the world to visit. The institution is connected in some way to almost all of the buildings featured here, via their designers, their commissioners, their influences, their locations. During the last decade, 30 per cent of nominees for the Turner Prize, the most notorious, controversial, contentious and polarising cultural award in the UK, have been alumni of the Glasgow School of Art. Four winners have been GSA graduates, with another the front-runner for the 2014 awards.

While this book was in the latter stages of being written, the devastating news broke of a fire at GSA. The iconic 'hen run' and the internationally acclaimed library were severely damaged. To many, the fire caused an intensely emotional reaction; the building is more than just stones and mortar. While money and human endeavour can conserve and restore much, the 'patina of age' and memories embedded in historic interiors add a quality to the spaces we inhabit that we cannot recreate. This brought to the fore the fragility of the buildings we love, and the realisation that we sometimes take them for granted until it is too late. Miraculously, 70 per cent of the interior and 90 per cent of the exterior were saved through the brave actions of the city's firefighters.

Several of the most famous and popular buildings featured within this book, including the City Chambers and Central Hotel, along with GSA, were proposed for demolition in the 1940s, following the controversial

Bruce Report, which recommended rebuilding most of the city centre as part of a modernisation plan. Much decoration within residential tenements, particularly tiles and glass, has been destroyed over the past 50 years. But, despite losses, Glasgow has retained substantial parts of its Victorian-built heritage; it still retains, for example, a greater proportion of its historic domestic glass than any other city in Britain. A wealth of our fragile heritage endures; however there is still work to be done to highlight, promote and protect Glasgow's unique interiors. The more fully they are appreciated, the more we can hope to safeguard what remains for the future.

Buildings here are organised by type and chronologically, and this tells its own story. While there were many other buildings Neale and I would have loved to include, if we could have, we have opened the doors to some for you and we hope you enjoy it.

Helen Kendrick
September 2014

Villas and Mansions

Pollok House

Pollok House, an ancestral stately home in the beautiful grounds of Pollok Country Park, was built around 250 years ago for wealthy landowners, the Maxwell family. It is now open to visitors under the management of the National Trust for Scotland and, perhaps inevitably, is referred to as 'Scotland's answer to Downton Abbey', offering guests an atmospheric glimpse into life in a grand period home.

The house's lavish interiors display the wealth and prosperity of the Maxwells. The triple-aspect music room features Ionic columns, intricate cornicing and grand arches framing the different views out onto the estate. The house is full of rare and evocative features such as the tin-glazed tiles in the guest suite, thought to have been made by Glasgow's Delftfield Pottery and dating from the mid-1700s. One of the house's most beguiling secrets is the magnificent Spanish art collection, widely recognised as the best in the UK, including works by El Greco and Goya.

As was the case with many large residential properties across the UK, Pollok House was used as a hospital for the wounded during the First World War, but there is little surviving evidence to show exactly how the building was re-appropriated during this time.

In true Downton style, the lower floors originally housed the servants'

Date: 1747–52, adapted 1890–1904

Original architect: William Adam; later adaptations, Robert Rowand Anderson

Address: Pollok Country Park

Status: A-listed

Original purpose: residential

Opposite. The grand entrance hall.

1

The music room features Ionic columns, intricate cornicing and arches to frame the multiple views onto the estate from the triple-aspect windows.

quarters and kitchen; the old store rooms, winding corridors, pantries and kitchens are a total contrast to the (albeit slightly faded) grandeur of upstairs. The kitchen now serves as a public cafe with servants' rooms and stores converted into shops and evocative display spaces.

The National Trust for Scotland was set up in 1931 in the ground-floor library of Pollok House, in a meeting convened by the house's owner, Sir John Stirling Maxwell. Fittingly, the property has been managed by the NTS since 1998. The NTS have a conservation philosophy for interiors of

favouring minimum intervention, ongoing conservation and damage limitation rather than overt restoration, thereby maintaining as much of the original, authentic materials and design in their care as possible.

The Maxwell family, owners of the Pollok estate for over 700 years, gifted the property, its unparalleled art collection and more than 350 acres of parkland to the city of Glasgow in 1966. They keep a personal apartment on the top floor of the house, and Sir John Maxwell-Macdonald and family are still in residence when in Glasgow.

Opposite. The house displays a collection of paintings, including what is widely recognised as the best Spanish art collection in the UK, featuring works by El Greco and Goya.

Above left. The magnificent entrance hall gives visitors a taste of life in a grand stately home of the eighteenth century.

Above right. The kitchen has been transformed into the house's restaurant. Details such as the copper pans on the wall, original range stove and shiny wall tiles are straight out of a Georgian doll's house.

Clifton

The Southside suburb of Pollokshields contains some spectacular historic villas, and Clifton is among the most impressive of them all. Originally commissioned by Glasgow businessman William Costigane as a family home, 'Clifton Hall', as it was originally known, was built by Pollokshields-dwelling architect John Gordon (also responsible for a number of warehouses for Costigane and the nearby Millar and Lang Publishing House, see pp. 53–57). The arresting floor-to-ceiling stained glass in the hallway, depicting the Trojan tale of Helen and Paris, was designed by Charles Gow, famed Glasgow stained-glass artist and former partner of Daniel Cottier (see Cottier's, pp. 109–113).

In the 1920s, the villa was bought and transformed into Elmtree Nursing Home and Maternity Hospital, later becoming a retirement and care home for the elderly.

In the early 2000s, changes in legislation meant Elmtree was no longer deemed suitable for use as a care home and it was sold. It was imagined that because of the scale of the property it would likely be split into flats, but in 2010 it was purchased by the current owner and carefully restored once more to a grand family home. Some of those involved in recent renovation works had stories of parents being born in the maternity wing, and subsequently living out their final days there in its role as a retirement home, highlighting the historical significance of the building for the local community.

Date: 1892

Architect: John Gordon

Address: Dalziel Drive

Status: B-listed

Original purpose: residential

Opposite. Formerly used as both a maternity hospital and a retirement home, the villa has played a central role in the local history of Pollokshields.

Right. The dramatic floor-to-ceiling windows by prominent stained-glass artist Charles Gow recount the story of Helen of Troy.

Opposite. The Corinthian columns, striking ceiling plasterwork and large windows combine to create a sense of grandeur in the lounge.

The modern stained glass, installed during the most recent phase of renovations of the property back to a family home, depicts a view of Loch Long from Tighnabruaich and juxtaposes with Gow's historic glass.

Somersby

Date: 1902

Architect: H.E. Clifford

Address: Dalziel Drive

Status: B-listed

Original purpose: residential

Opposite. The drawing room, originally used as the billiard room, features dramatic oak trussing and beams.

Somersby is a rare example in Glasgow of residential Arts & Crafts architecture. It was built in 1902 for oil and produce broker W.T. Geddes by the architect H.E. Clifford, renowned in the city for his Glasgow Style tenements, the A-listed Pollokshields Burgh Halls and the dramatic, mystical villa of Stoneleigh on Cleveden Drive, Kelvinside.

Clifford was one of only a few Scottish architects to feature in Hermann Muthesius's definitive 1905 book on nineteenth-century domestic architecture, *Das englische Haus*, and Somersby itself featured in the seminal design magazine *The Studio* in 1908, illustrating the building's significance on a international scale. Both *Das englische Haus* and *The Studio* promoted the work of 'new art' artists, designers and architects; they both featured Charles Rennie Mackintosh and were influential publications in Europe, playing a key role in disseminating the work of UK designers of the period.

The design for the art nouveau rug in Somersby's reception area was taken from the binding of a 1901 book, *Celtic Fairy Tales*, designed by Edith de Rheims. De Rheims was a member of the international Guild of Women Binders, a prestigious designers' collective that ran from 1898 to1904 and favoured the art nouveau style. The distinctive Arts & Crafts fireplace in the drawing room was bought at auction; it is thought to have come from 4 Great Western Terrace, the grand Alexander Thomson-designed townhouse (see pp. 17–22).

The house has been painstakingly restored by current owner Ann Laing, whose eye for detail, knowledge of the Arts & Crafts/Glasgow Style aesthetic, and passion for historic interiors has added much to the beauty of the house.

The vaulted ceiling of the upper hallway, decorated in black-and-white chequerboard, adds an idiosyncratic touch to the elegant space.

The reception room, showing the beautiful fireplace and specially commissioned art nouveau-inspired carpet.

Townhouses

4 Great Western Terrace

Reading about a Glasgow-based architect from the late 1800s cited as 'one of the great forerunners of the Modern movement', one might presume the architect in question to be Charles Rennie Mackintosh. But this accolade has been used by scholars to describe Alexander Greek Thomson, well known as Glasgow's 'other' world-class architect, and argued by many in the city to be superior to his more high-profile successor, CRM. While his *oeuvre* may be less internationally acclaimed, Thomson's masterworks, such as Egyptian Halls and Holmwood House, are firmly on the Scottish architectural map. Thomson had a prolific career and produced a diverse range of structures, including a castle, tenements, three churches and several urbane terraces, including Great Western Terrace.

Of the kilometre of grand terraces stretching across the southern aspect of Great Western Road, Great Western Terrace has been called the most 'severe and monumental', elevated from its neighbouring blocks on a raised platform and accessed via imposing steps and ramps at each end. Inside No. 4, the monumentalism continues with vast rooms, dramatic features such as the dining-room window arch and the bold decorative scheme, using elaborate patterns and a daring colour palette.

Alexander Thomson obtained the moniker 'Greek Thomson' due to

Date: 1869

Architect: Alexander Thomson

Address:
4 Great Western Terrace

Status: A-listed

Original purpose: residential

Opposite. The view of the entrance hall from the first-floor gallery showcases the classical Ionic columns and decorative mosaic tiled floor.

Right. The dining room features the kind of stained-glass window and elaborate stone archway more commonly found in ecclesiastic architecture.

Opposite. The stairwell, leading from the grand reception area to the first-floor gallery, top-lit by a grand cupola, includes exotic detailing in the cast-iron balustrade.

his utilisation of motifs and stylistic elements from Greece and Egypt, designing buildings of an 'exotic, haunting strangeness' that brought both classicism and originality to the city. He never actually visited Greece and, unlike some of his contemporaries who travelled widely in Europe and America, when he died in 1875 he'd never left the UK. But as an architect with an artistic and philosophical bent, he read widely and drew much influence from what was happening in international circles through journals, books and international visitors to Scotland.

A large-scale conservation project of No. 4, grant-aided by Historic Scotland, was undertaken in the 1990s, restoring the building's interior to its original splendour. It happily (but unusually) remains one integral property, serving as a rare reminder of the family homes the well-heeled West End Victorians enjoyed.

Opposite. Details such as the exotic door-furniture add to the drama of the room.

Left. The distinctive wall decoration in the lounge includes gold stencilled wall-coverings.

22 Park Circus

'The most exquisite interiors in the West End, if not the city, its only rival being City Chambers,' comments Carol Foreman in her book *Hidden Glasgow* about 22 Park Circus, an iconic, and distinctly Glaswegian, part of the city's built heritage. Many in the city are familiar with the property through its use for the past twenty years (since 1994) as the city's registry office for civil marriages. Its lavish, opulent and imposing interiors provided a suitably monumental backdrop for the many weddings that took place there, and for the events that occurred during its former uses as a consulate, the Casa d'Italia, Glasgow's Italian cultural centre and, originally, a home.

In 1872, local cast-iron magnate Walter Macfarlane, creator of the internationally significant Saracen Foundry, commissioned a home in the salubrious new Park district, well situated for its elevated position to the west of the city and for access to the adjacent West End Park (now known as Kelvingrove Park). James Boucher, a local architect who had also designed two of Macfarlane's city foundries, in Anderston and the monumental premises at Possilpark, was commissioned for the job. Boucher had undertaken a grand tour of Europe in recent years and his home for Macfarlane displays many European influences: Renaissance stairwells, imposing vaulted corridors lined with marble Corinthian columns and highly decorative anterooms.

Macfarlane never had children, but his 'adopted son', his nephew (also named Walter), moved into the property in 1898 and soon after commissioned local architects James Salmon and John 'Gaff' Gillespie to undertake work on the property. Salmon and Gillespie were purveyors of the Glasgow Style and there are several art nouveau touches throughout the building, including stunning tiles, glasswork, fireplaces and a cast-iron conservatory. Stephen Adam Junior was also brought in to design the beautiful stained glass for one of the art nouveau fireplace surrounds.

In 1934, following Walter Junior's death, the home became an Italian cultural club, the Casa d'Italia, purchased through public donations from

Date: 1872–4

Architect: James Boucher

Address: 22 Park Circus

Status: A-listed

Original purpose: residential

Opposite. The entrance corridor of this grand former townhouse features marble columns, intricate plasterwork and dramatic cupolas.

the Scottish–Italian community. The club leased some of its space to the Italian consulate and it became a regional hub for Italians in the city. Unfortunately, it was not financially sustainable and the property was sold to developers in 1990, when the Casa was declared bankrupt. A large-scale conservation project was undertaken before the building was leased to the Glasgow City Council as the registry office.

At the time of writing the property is for sale, and the future of this A-listed city icon hangs in the air. The building has proved highly adaptable since its construction; what happens next will be followed with much interest.

Opposite. The first-floor gallery and grand cupola, featuring fish scale glazing.

Left. Glasgow Style architects Salmon and Gillespie brought several art nouveau touches to the interior, including this stunning fireplace, with stained glass by Stephen Adam Junior.

Lochgarry House

Date: 1904–5

Architect: J.C. McKellar

Address: Cleveden Drive

Status: B-listed

Original purpose: residential

Opposite. A curved glass extension integrates the garden into the historic house. (Photograph: Andrew Lee)

This beautiful townhouse in the leafy Kelvinside area of Glasgow was built by the Glasgow-born architect John McKellar in the early part of the twentieth century. At the age of just twenty-four, McKellar set up his own architectural practice specialising in tenement building. Soon after establishing his practice, he set out to design a residential terrace of five houses on Cleveden Drive (called Montgomerie Drive at the time) and, as often happens with the best domestic projects, one of the properties, this one, subsequently became the architect's home.

The house was in use as a council-funded boys' home until the early 1990s, when it was deemed to be unsuitable for this purpose, and in 2009 the property had a multimillion-pound redevelopment by Archial architects to reconfigure it into its current incarnation as a modern family home. Period features, including the stunning stained glass, have been maintained, while ultra-modern features such as the glass staircase and extension have been added. The conversion won the Roses Design Award in 2010.

Right. The hallway juxtaposes beautiful historic features, including Glasgow Style stained glass and timber wall panelling with the contemporary stairway. (Photograph: Andrew Lee)

Opposite. The grand Edwardian scale of the original architecture has been brought firmly into the twenty-first century with a new, ultramodern kitchen and mezzanine. (Photograph: Andrew Lee)

Tenements

Albany Mansions

Albany Mansions, a four-storey red-sandstone tenement block just off the main intersection of Charing Cross, is a true hidden gem. This idiosyncratic building was designed by Glasgow superstar architect J.J. Burnet, also responsible for Clydeport (see pp. 41–45) and perhaps the more well-known Charing Cross Mansions just over the road.

Born in Glasgow and trained as an architect at his father's practice, in 1872 Burnet studied in Paris at the École des Beaux-Arts. He went on to travel extensively in Europe and America, and is often discussed as bringing a Parisian style to Glasgow, with his elegant classical yet modern approach, as demonstrated here at Albany Mansions and in buildings such as the Athenaeum on Buchanan Street.

Up until the 1890s, residential tenement facade design was largely classical and unadorned (with a major exception being found in the work of Alexander Thomson). However, by the 1890s, and coincident with the introduction of red sandstone in the city, the streetscape began to change. The popular trend in London for 'mansion flats' had been introduced there from Scotland by Norman Shaw and it rebounded back to Glasgow. The city's architects, some of whom had now studied and travelled in the grand cities of Europe, began to include more elaborate details in tenement

Date: c.1896

Architect:
John James Burnet

Address: Renfrew Street

Status: B-listed

Original purpose: residential

Opposite. The style of doors in the close is unusual, with the two sitting at diagonals and each door opening into a designated recess behind, giving a luxurious feeling of additional space on entering. The landings and entrance corridor in the close feature beautiful mosaic flooring.

facades. The tenements were recast as heroically scaled luxury apartments and included corner turrets, communal walkways, sculptural pediments and, as seen here at Albany Mansions, elegant balconies.

Albany Mansions has a close physical proximity to the Glasgow School of Art, and J.J. Burnet is said to have helped Charles Rennie Mackintosh win the contract to design what is now internationally renowned as the latter's masterwork, a stylistic precursor to the modernist movement and the building that put Glasgow, and Mackintosh, firmly on the architectural map.

One of the flats within Albany Mansions was designed specifically as an artist's residence. Soon after building was complete it was occupied by the painter John McGhie, who had links with Burnet through a shared history of attending the École des Beaux Arts; and later by the young artist Annie Low and her architect husband James Laing, a contemporary of Burnet who also travelled and studied extensively on the Continent. The flat itself features a double–height galleried living room, with a gallery leading to the designated studio above it, huge skylights flooding the space with preferred northern light. An unusual and enchanting aspect of the flat is a top–floor roof garden, giving private, secluded outside space amongst the rooftops, a rarity in the densely built-up heart of the city.

A Wally Close

From the mid-1800s onwards, tenement housing sprang up in Glasgow to house the mass influx of workers to the Second City of the Empire. While stories and archival photography of tenements in the east of the city during this time describe their infamous squalor, the tenements of the West End were altogether different. These, built for the city's academics, artists, merchants, rich industrialists and wealthy bohemians, displayed grand proportions, intricate decorative plasterwork, panelling, stained glass, beautiful tiling on the floors and walls of reception areas, elegant bay windows and decorative stonework, commonly in the Glasgow Style.

Often the grander tenements in the West End would include internally what is referred to locally as a 'Wally Close': the decoratively tiled public area of the tenement (the term 'wally' comes from the Old Scots word meaning 'pale ceramic'). Rather than the communal reception areas of the tenement being painted, as in more modest properties, Wally Closes were tiled with decorative, beautifully coloured ceramic tiles with Glasgow Style motifs, extending usually up to the first floor or in some cases all the way to the top. Not every district in Glasgow had these Wally Closes, and they were regarded as extremely desirable, with oral histories recording residents' stories of communal cleaning sessions every Friday night. The ceramic tiles, as well as looking beautiful and having a distinctly tactile quality were also practical and hard-wearing; many Wally Closes have survived more than a hundred years of daily use and still look (almost) as pristine as they were originally.

Along with the tiling in the Wally Closes, the communal glass (the windows of the communal stairwells and the glass in the individual front doors) was highly decorative. Between 1870 and 1914, Glasgow was an important centre for the production of stained glass, with some of Europe's most innovative artistic producers, such as Stephen Adam Jnr, George Walton, W.G. Morton and E.A. Taylor, designing glass in the Glasgow Style for homes in the city.

While the days of communal cleaning may be over, there is still a pride

Date: 1900

Original purpose: residential

Opposite. Tiles in an original 'Wally Close'.

Above. Wally close tiles in Glasgow often feature decorative motifs from nature.

Opposite. Tenements throughout the city often displayed beautiful tiling on the walls of the communal areas.

in and high levels of desirability for the Wally Closes. Residents speak with great affection of the tiles and stained glass; of opening the front doors on dark, rainy winter nights to see the exquisite glossy tiles and coloured windows glowing under the electric lights. Visitors to the city are often astonished to see such intricately decorative communal areas in a tenement. The huge variety of colours and detailing in the tiles (such as motifs of ships, which can be found in some Wally Closes), directly reflects not only the surrounding natural environment but also the city's rich industrial heritage within the domestic interior.

Offices

Clydeport

Often cited as among the most impressive of all Glasgow interiors by the relatively few who have been inside, Clydeport remains private offices for its trustees and is seldom open to the public.

Built from Giffnock stone, with a polished granite base, the exterior of the building is immediately arresting, with sculptures of ships by the famed John Mossman protruding from either side of the entrance, and Neptune and Amphitrite above, by Albert Hodge. On entering, the dramatic stained glass in the stairwell immediately takes centre stage, with imagery telling stories of shipbuilding, fishing, engineering and biblical tales.

The first-storey corridor, with its beautiful tiled floor, elaborate Corinthian columns and distinctive stained glass, is similar to Glasgow City Chambers (see pp. 77–83), which was being built simultaneously with Clydeport. It is fitting that a comparable level of grandeur and opulence to that shown within the headquarters of the city council was employed for the Clyde Trust's offices, demonstrating the historic importance of the River Clyde and the wealth and opportunities it brought to the city.

All the decorative glass within the building is by Stephen Adam, one of the city's most renowned stained-glass artists, whose work can be found across Glasgow, including within City Chambers and Maryhill Burgh

Date: 1883–6, extended 1906–8

Architect:
John James Burnet

Address:
16 Robertson Street

Status: A-listed

Original purpose: offices

Opposite. The dramatic Trust Hall.

Halls (pp. 71–75). Edinburgh-born Adam set up a studio in Glasgow in 1870 and was one of the most prolific and significant stained-glass artists in the country for the next forty years until his death in 1910. Alongside artists such as Daniel Cottier, Adam is internationally renowned as a pioneer in the field of progressive stained-glass art.

Aside from the stunning glass, the sculpture and decorative plasterwork throughout, and specifically in the Trustees Room, is outstanding, featuring gilded goddesses and an elaborate cupola surround. Burnet had a hand in much of the interior design and furniture for the offices, which contributes to the integrity and impressiveness of the internal spaces. The building is open for public tours during the city's annual Doors Open Day festival, allowing visitors a rare glimpse inside this historic treasure.

Opposite. J.J. Burnet also designed much of the interior and furniture for the offices, which contributes to the integrity and unique character of the building.

Right. All the decorative glass within the building is by Stephen Adam, perhaps the city's most renowned stained-glass artist, whose work can be found across the city.

Fairfield Shipyard Offices

Date: 1890

Architect: John Keppie

Address: 1048 Govan Road

Status: A-listed

Original purpose: offices

Opposite. The mosaic floor and elegant arches of the entrance. The letters 'GS' stand for Govan Shipbuilders.

Fairfield Shipyard Offices in Govan served as the main offices for the eponymous shipyard, famous the world over during the late nineteenth and early twentieth centuries for producing grand ocean liners, luxurious steamers and naval ships. Fairfield was known as the 'jewel in the crown' of the Clyde's prosperous shipbuilding industry – until the post-war downturn in industry and subsequent economic decline of the area.

The Fairfield Shipyard Offices, an architectural symbol of the city's rich nautical heritage, ceased to have an active function in 2001; the premises sat vacant and fell into disrepair until 2010, when they were taken on by Govan Workspace, a local social enterprise. One of Govan's grandest buildings, this category A-listed site has recently benefitted from a multimillion-pound regeneration project to transform it into a workspace for businesses and a local heritage centre.

Many famous vessels, including ships for both world wars, were built at Fairfield, the largest and most successful shipyard on the Clyde. In 1912, at the height of the yard's prosperity, twelve ships were commissioned in that single year. Today, Fairfield is one of only two remaining merchant shipyards in Glasgow.

The office building itself, designed by architect John Keppie in 1890, has dramatic interior features including an oak-panelled boardroom, intricate mosaic floors and an open-plan top floor studio flooded with light from triple-aspect windows and skylights.

Over £1.5 million of emergency repairs to the office building were carried out in recent years to make it watertight, including refurbishing all of its existing 162 windows. Eleven office suites, encompassing more than 18,000 square feet, and 3,000 square feet of publicly accessible heritage space on the ground floor, exploring the history of shipbuilding and its relationship with the Govan community, have also been added.

Pat Cassidy, managing director of Govan Workspace, has heard many interesting tales from people with a relationship to Fairfield: 'Our visitors have all sorts of connection to the offices,' he says. 'For example, we get

visitors who worked out the back in the shipyard their whole career but had never come into the main building. The foreman would come in and get the wages and sort out all the paperwork, so the workers would live alongside this grand, iconic building but never go in. We're happy people can come and visit now, to finally see what was behind closed doors.'

Architectural historian Ranald MacInnes, head of heritage management for Historic Scotland, sees the Fairfield Shipyard Offices as a key symbol of what Scotland has always done well: innovate. 'Glasgow led the world in shipbuilding,' he comments, 'but in more recent years has become internationally renowned for the creative and successful reuse of our historic buildings. Whereas the Fairfield office building may at one point have been a painful reminder of the decline of such a successful industrial past in Govan, it now stands as a symbol of a new way in which Scotland is leading the world: heritage-led regeneration. We have reconnected with our industrial past and can be proud of it.'

The current restoration of Fairfield Shipyard Offices is a crucial part of the wider regeneration of the area. Govan has a rich and diverse built heritage stretching back to early Christian times, including many iconic nineteenth-century buildings.

Overleaf. The light-flooded former drawing room on the upper level has been transformed into modern office space.

Millar and Lang Publishing House

Charles Rennie Mackintosh's art nouveau designs are internationally famous. His motifs have spawned many contemporary homages in the form of glass, jewellery and furniture, which are available for sale across the world. However, art nouveau interior decoration in Glasgow is not the sole preserve of Mackintosh and some of the most stunning original examples of the city's interpretation of the style lie hidden away in the everyday interiors of Glasgow's tenements, offices and bars. A former publishing house in Pollokshields displays what is perhaps one of the most striking collections of art nouveau interior decoration in Scotland and yet there are few who know it is there.

Designed in 1901 by D.B. Dobson of Gordon and Dobson, the building was originally the premises of Millar and Lang, city art publishers. The front of the building is unmistakably Glasgow Style, with some Mackintosh-esque detailing in the sculpture and sinuous curved architrave above the doorway. But the real beauty of the building is revealed once inside the front door. The building is A-listed, largely, to quote Historic Scotland, due to its 'fine and exceptionally complete Art Nouveau interiors'.

The public hallway has beautiful wall tiles, flooring and door furniture, and there is evidence of missing glazing.

On entering the first-floor offices, a dramatic stained-glass screen designed by W.G. Morton welcomes you, depicting a striking selection of nautical imagery, including ships, seahorses, whales, dolphins and Neptune. Elsewhere there are mosaics of naked nymphs and mermaids, and brass door furniture, including handles and finger plates, all heavily enriched with art nouveau detail. Perching above the toilet doors, there is also an intricate marble sculpture of a dragon, whose eyes can allegedly be illuminated with electric light (although the current tenants joke no one is quite sure where the switch is).

Date: 1901

Architect: John Gordon/ D.B. Dobson

Address: Darnley Street

Status: A-listed

Original purpose: offices

Opposite. The dramatic 1902 glass screen designed by W.G. Morton in the reception area of this former art publishers depicts a striking selection of nautical imagery.

Right. The entrance area of the former art publishers maintains its original art nouveau tiles, mosaic floors, stained glass, marble sculptures and door furniture.

Opposite. The internal doors feature beautiful stained glass and intricately detailed brass door furniture.

Opposite. The glossy ceramic wall tiles feature motifs from nature.

Left. A mosaic of a water nymph greets visitors in the entrance foyer of the building.

Hotels

Blythswood Square Hotel

Blythswood Square, the home of the glamorous five-star eponymous hotel, is one of the finest examples in the city of classical Georgian architecture. The square was originally designed as four identical terraces of townhouses in a quadrangle with central gardens. In 1910, the eastern stretch of townhouses became the clubhouse for the Royal Scottish Automobile Club (RSAC). The club purchased all the houses and commissioned the eminent James Miller (most famous for his designs for Glasgow's Central Station) to remodel the whole terrace as the club headquarters.

The redevelopment was completed in 1926, leaving the RSAC with an elegant and comfortable venue, where according to the fashionable press of the time, 'most of Glasgow's business community would meet'. The RSAC sold the property in 2002 and it was then converted into a hotel; now the bar and spa facilities are popular with local business people and, as such, this tradition as a central meeting place endures.

As well as being a key location for businesses such as legal and financial offices, Blythswood Square has a history as the city's centre of 'the world's oldest profession', with the area by the late twentieth century having the greatest concentration of prostitutes in Scotland. The Blythswood Hotel wittily references this aspect of its location's social history with its use of red lights in the front-facing windows.

Date: 1821–3, adapted 1923–6

Architect attr.: William Burn and George Smith; adaptations: James Miller

Address: 11 Blythswood Square

Status: B-listed

Original purpose: residential

Opposite. The Blythswood Hotel reception. (Photograph: Renzo Mazzolini)

Overleaf. The sweeping marble staircase. (Photograph: Renzo Mazzolini)

1 Devonshire Gardens

Date: c.1870

Architect: unknown

Address:
1–5 Devonshire Gardens

Status: B-listed

Original purpose:
residential

Opposite. The main entrance combines marble columns, an intricate mosaic floor, wood panelling, decorative cornice work, a grand sweeping staircase and stained glass to dramatic effect.

This grand terrace of five former townhouses now forms the luxury hotel unofficially known as 1 Devonshire Gardens, part of the Hotel du Vin group. House numbers 1–3 were first amalgamated into a hotel in 1986, followed by No. 5, then most recently (in 2006) No. 4 was acquired as the 'final piece of the jigsaw', allowing the entire terrace to become one integral unit.

Until 1902, No. 4 was home to Sir William Burrell, Glasgow shipping magnate, avid art collector and philanthropist. He commissioned George Walton (an important cast member in the story of the city's art and design history) to design the stained-glass windows in the stairwell.

Walton, an alumnus of the Glasgow School of Art and a contemporary of Charles Rennie Mackintosh, had some high-profile and wealthy clients in Glasgow throughout his career, including Burrell and also Miss Cranston, famous tearoom proprietress, for whom he designed the interiors for the Argyle Street and Buchanan Street tearooms.

Walton was heavily influenced by James Whistler and William Morris, and helped to pioneer the Glasgow Style, the city's distinctive interpretation of art nouveau. When Burrell later moved two blocks east to No. 8 Great Western Terrace, he again commissioned Walton to design the glass for his new home, some of which still survives.

The hotel at Devonshire Gardens now embraces its history as former townhouses, with public rooms recreating the atmosphere of a grand family home. There is a private, leafy garden to the rear of the hotel, a welcome rarity in the compact West End, complete with treehouse-style humidor for those requiring a post-prandial cigar. The hotel in its various guises has played host to high-profile guests over the years from Princess Anne to Kylie.

Opposite. The dramatic stained glass at No. 4 was designed by George Walton.

Above left. The hotel lounge demonstrates the hotel's informal 'home from home' atmosphere.

Above right. The hotel interior features art nouveau elements, including fireplace and mirror, showing influence from European designers such as Louis Majorelle.

Grand Central Hotel

Known as the grande dame of Glasgow hotels, the Grand Central Hotel at Central Station harnesses the romance and excitement of the railway age, the majestic architecture of the station itself and the air of anticipation that comes with crowds arriving and departing to create a truly atmospheric spot in the city.

The hotel was originally designed by Robert Rowand Anderson, the Edinburgh architect also responsible for Mount Stuart House on Bute and the founder of the Royal Incorporation of Architects in Scotland, who had travelled and studied widely in Europe. Anderson was also responsible for the interior design of some of the public rooms, and stunning details such as the elaborate cornicing, marble columns and gilded cupolas survive. The hotel was completed in 1883 but was extended, along with the station, in 1901–6 by James Miller (see Blythswood Square Hotel, pp. 59–61), reopening to great aplomb in 1907.

The hotel has had some illustrious guests during its days, including Frank Sinatra, Mae West and Charlie Chaplin, and has been privy to some historic occasions – the world's first long-distance television pictures were transmitted to the Central Hotel in 1927 by John Logie Baird.

In the latter half of the twentieth century, the grandeur started to fade and multiple owners of the hotel failed to make it a financial success. It subsequently closed in 2009, amid concerns of asbestos contamination and structural deterioration. Happily, a £20 million renovation programme commenced and in autumn 2010 the hotel reopened as the four-star Grand Central. It is now a popular place for weddings, conferences and festive events; a seat in the first floor Champagne Bar, overlooking Central Station's concourse, is a prime spot for those waiting with anticipation for their guests to arrive on the train.

A large proportion of the hotel's overnight guests come from central Scotland, illustrating its appeal amongst immediate neighbours and ex-locals of the city, as an iconically 'Glasgow' place to stay when visiting.

Date: 1883; extension 1901–6

Architect:
Robert Rowand Anderson;
 extension, James Miller

Address: Central Station,
99 Gordon Street

Status: A-listed

Original purpose: hotel

Opposite. The bar features a dramatic gilded dome cupola surrounded by Ionic marble columns and intricate cornicing.

Opposite. The bold
contemporary chandelier
emphasises the scale of
the grand staircase.

Above. The floor of the public bar was
'hidden' for many years under fixtures
and fittings but was restored in the
most recent phase of refurbishment.

Civic and Municipal Buildings

Maryhill Burgh Halls

'The burgh of Maryhill presents few attractions to the rambler in search of the picturesque' – while this description of Maryhill from an 1878 edition of the *Glasgow Herald* may have been written over 130 years ago, it might be suggested by some that it still rings true today. A recent multimillion-pound heritage regeneration programme for the area, however, means it is undergoing something of a cultural renaissance and the restoration of Maryhill Burgh Halls is central in the project. The Halls were out of full-time use for many years, derelict and empty, with various projects to regenerate them never fully successful. From 2003, the building was on the city's 'Buildings at Risk' register, with its future looking uncertain.

Maryhill became an independent burgh in 1857. The town grew rapidly, and the original municipal buildings quickly became too small for requirements. As a result, a complex of new municipal buildings was commissioned at the corner of Maryhill Road and Gairbraid Avenue, opening in 1878. The buildings initially comprised the Burgh Halls, offices for police commissioners and a police station incorporating 'Fifteen cells, four of which have been specially designed for the accommodation of "drunks".' The site was later extended, adding a fire station (incorporating a tenement above for the firemen to live in), and later still, a complex of

Date: 1878

Architect:
Duncan McNaughtan

Address:
10 Gairbraid Avenue

Status: B-listed

Original purpose:
municipal building

Opposite. Maryhill Burgh Halls were originally built as municipal buildings.
(Photograph: Andrew Lee)

baths and washhouses. All are now listed buildings.

Architectural historian Gordon Barr, who led the project to restore the building, comments: 'When you start to look more closely at Maryhill, and despite the best efforts of Glasgow's town planners to destroy much of its built heritage in the 1970s, the area has retained a surprising number of historic and architecturally significant buildings, including Mackintosh's Queen's Cross Church and Ruchill Church Halls . . . But the real jewel in the crown for me are the Maryhill municipal buildings – with baths, washhouses, a fire station, police station, and especially the Maryhill Burgh Halls, with their unique stained-glass panels.'

These twenty stained-glass windows show a selection of the trades, industries and occupations of the area. They were commissioned from the studio of Adam and Small – run by Stephen Adam, one of the foremost practitioners of the art at the time, whose work can be seen all over Glasgow. It is largely the realism of the portrayals of industries and trades in the Maryhill windows that makes these panels so unique in the city; they are in marked contrast to Stephen Adam's other stained-glass treatments of similar subjects. His windows for Glasgow City Chambers (1882–90), for example, include depictions of workmen, but they are portrayed in classical clothing and poses; in contrast, the windows at Maryhill show the subjects in their contemporary everyday working clothes, not dressed up or stylised. A range of different occupations are represented, from the traditional (joiners, blacksmiths) to the industrial (iron moulding, gas workers) and the professional (a teacher in his classroom, soldiers at Maryhill Barracks). Unusually, two of the panels also feature female workers (calico printers and linen bleachers). The glass panels provide a glimpse into the social and industrial heritage of the area and offer a reminder, when looking at men pouring molten metal or working in a sawmill with little or no protective clothing, of the relaxed attitudes of the period towards health and safety.

The stained glass was removed from the building in the 1960s and remained in the care of Glasgow Museums until, as part of the recent restoration, a number of the original panels were once again put on display in the building in which they were designed to be seen.

Glasgow City Chambers

In the heart of the city, the City Chambers' distinctive domed tower and grand stone facade provide the backdrop to a thousand tourist photographs and diverse cultural events throughout the year, and they are still used as originally intended as a suitably prestigious home for the headquarters of Glasgow City Council. Famous for its opulence, City Chambers is an architectural gem and has witnessed some fascinating episodes in Glasgow's past. The exterior is embellished with detailed sculpture, reflecting Victorian Glasgow's status as the Second City of the Empire. Each carving tells a story, and Glasgow's trades and industries are all represented in panels by John Mossman.

Despite the grandness of the exterior, all is not as it seems: the imposing sandstone conceals a brick structure (albeit built from ten million bricks). However, no expense was spared in creating the lavish interior; the budget was controversially increased to a massive (at the time) £500,000. The Chambers' interior is one of the most extraordinary in the city, if not the country. Ceilings decorated with gold leaf, mosaic floors and a sweeping, polished white Carrara marble staircase (reputedly the biggest marble staircase in the world) are flooded with light from huge stained-glass domes above. Lavish light fittings, alabaster and carved mahogany panelling and Italian glazed tiling add to the opulence.

Despite being an important Glasgow landmark, the City Chambers was nearly demolished as part of a post-war plan to modernise the city. The Bruce Report proposed the demolition of Glasgow city centre in its entirety – the City Chambers was not the only potential victim. Kelvingrove Museum and Art Gallery, Glasgow School of Art and Central Station were all earmarked for destruction. Thankfully, the plan was not actioned: Glasgow has been said to have the finest surviving Victorian cityscape in the world.

Public tours of the A-listed City Chambers are conducted twice a day and the building continues to play an important role in Glasgow life, for those who live and work in the city, as well as for those many tourists who visit each year.

Date: 1882–8

Architect: William Young

Address: George Square

Status: A-listed

Original purpose: municipal building

Opposite. There are only two places in western Europe with full marble staircases: Glasgow's City Chambers and the Vatican in Rome. City Chambers has indeed been used as the Vatican in several films.

Overleaf. The stunning Banqueting Hall features many paintings by Glasgow artists depicting historic scenes of the city.

Left. The exquisite faience tiles in the councillors' corridor are from Burmantofts, one of the premier tile manufacturers in Europe of the period, based in Leeds (see also Cup Tea Lounge, pp. 142–147).

Opposite and p. 80. The third-floor picture gallery features portraits of all the city's Provosts from the past 150 years.

Right. The mosaic floor in the grand entrance hall features the official Glasgow motto: 'Let Glasgow Flourish'.

Entertainment Venues

Britannia Panopticon Music Hall

The Britannia Panopticon is one of the finest surviving early music halls in the world. Originally built as a department store for the city's growing middle class, the somewhat raucous nature of its east-end locale did not lend itself to that purpose so well and it was proposed that a music hall would perhaps be more suitable. This proved to be a canny suggestion and it succeeded as a music hall and entertainment venue until 1938, when the doors were finally closed.

Built by Gildard and Macfarlane Architects in 1857 in the 'Italian Palazzo' style, when the Britannia first opened acts consisted of dancing girls, comic singing and ballad singers. By the later 1860s, however, it had developed a reputation more for dancing girls than ballad singers, and it was regarded as one of the most salacious and debauched entertainment spots in Glasgow. The music hall was taken into a new era by Mr and Mrs Rossborough, who bought the building in 1869, shaking off the less-than-salubrious image and transforming it into one of the most successful entertainment venues in the city. Indeed, it was among the first properties in Glasgow to install electricity and subsequently became one of the earliest places in the city to put on animated picture shows.

By the turn of the twentieth century, the Britannia was no longer the

Date: 1857

Architect:
Gildard and Macfarlane

Address: 117 Trongate

Status: A-listed

Original purpose:
department store

Opposite. The main theatre area of the Britannia Panopticon.

The Britannia Panopticon
Music Hall has been packing
visitors in since the 1850s
and the theatre interior gives
a fascinating insight into
the history of popular
entertainment in Britain.

desirable destination developed by the Rossboroughs. In comparison with newer, competing attractions, like the Pavilion and the King's Theatre, it was starting to show its age. In 1906, it was taken over again, this time by impresario A.E Pickard. At this stage, the building entered one of its most colourful periods. Pickard closed for two weeks to renovate the building and on its grand re-opening it was re-named 'the Grand Panopticon' (the word Panopticon deriving from the Latin *pan* meaning 'everything' and *opti* meaning 'see').

Wax-work enthusiast Pickard proceeded to install a games arcade in the attic of the building and turned the basement into a zoo. In addition to this, there were rooms containing weird and wonderful attractions of

every description, from the world's tallest man to the world's ugliest woman.

Happily, the Britannia Panopticon is once again being used as it was originally intended and puts on a number of different performances, from stand-up during the comedy festival to burlesque dance shows.

The building is internationally significant and holds many clues for historians as to popular entertainment over the last 150 years and the cultural history of Glasgow. It has recently undergone a major series of repair and restoration works, with a further phase of work planned, to ensure this unique part of Glasgow's heritage is safeguarded for the future.

The Arlington Baths

Date: 1870–1

Architect: John Burnet Senior

Address: 61 Arlington Street

Status: A-listed

Original purpose:
swimming baths

Opposite. The exotic, turn-of-the-century Turkish Room at the Arlington.

The Arlington is the oldest community swimming club in the UK – and, some suggest, the world. Originally designed by John Burnet senior (not to be confused with his son John 'J.J.' Burnet, it is classical Italianate in exterior style, with traditional Victorian interiors. A sky-lit double-height pool hall, with its original acrobatic rings and trapeze, still present, provides the dramatic centrepiece.

The building had several major additions between 1875 and 1902 as the club moved with the times and incorporated new facilities. An exotic, tiled Turkish room, referred to as a 'Glaswegian homage to the Alhambra', was added, along with a billiard room and an upper storey to provide further space. These adaptations allowed the membership to grow and the club to remain at the forefront of popular trends.

As the well-heeled citizens of Glasgow began to move westwards from the city centre, the Arlington, just west of Charing Cross, tapped into a demand for a club where locals could gather to engage in sport, indulge in some relaxation time and socialise. The Victorians were highly class-conscious and would have enjoyed this opportunity to demonstrate their wealth and success; membership of a club such as this demonstrated their status as part of the 'leisured classes', with sophisticated, modern sensibilities.

Today, happily, the Arlington remains a thriving club in the community, providing its members with a blend of sport, relaxation space and sociability. The loyal membership of the much-loved not-for-profit club includes many whose families have been attending the baths for several generations, a testament to its enduring appeal. Along with the twenty-one-metre swimming pool, members can still enjoy the original historic features, including the option of a hot poolside bath in the original freestanding Victorian slipper tubs, big enough to share.

Right. The swimming pool retains its original acrobatic rings and trapeze.

Opposite. The original Victorian slipper tubs at the side of the pool are a popular feature of the historic club.

The Arches

The Arches is an arts and music venue, bar and nightclub situated in the previously derelict area below Glasgow Central railway station. This vast 6,000-metre square industrial space in the brick arches of the viaduct that leads into the station was converted to house the major exhibition 'Glasgow's Glasgow' during the 1990 European City of Culture celebrations. When the exhibition ended, the space was taken over with the intention to run it as an arts venue, and the two floors and seven subterranean brick arches leant themselves to conversion to a nightclub.

The turn-of-the-century industrial styling and scale of the interiors at the Arches give a unique atmosphere and it has become something of a cultural icon in Glasgow since its '90s transformation. As well as being a stunning example of Glasgow's industrial heritage and innovative reuse of space, the Arches is regularly voted amongst the best clubs in the world and continues to be a successful part of Glasgow's vibrant music, theatre and arts scene.

Date:
(station redevelopment)
1899–1905

Architect/Engineer:
Donald A. Matheson

Address: 253 Argyle Street

Status:
(Central Station) A-listed

Original purpose:
railway arches

Opposite. The main bar.

Far left. The previously derelict space was adapted in the 1990s.

Left. The Arches is now one of Europe's most famous nightclubs.

Glasgow Film Theatre

Date: 1938–9

Architect:
James McKissack

Address: 12 Rose Street

Status: B-listed

Original purpose: cinema

Opposite. The entrance area, corridors and mezzanine-level cafe feature art deco details throughout the original woodwork and an iconic streamline moderne bar.

Overleaf. Much of the original decoration has been retained, including the central light feature in Cinema 1, nicknamed 'Mr Cosmo's Bowler Hat' after the eponymous cartoon figure used in the cinema's publicity.

Between the 1920s and '30s, Glasgow was home to more than 130 cinemas. The city had more cinemas per person than any other place outside America and thus earned itself the moniker 'Cinema City'. The Cosmo Cinema (later to become the Glasgow Film Theatre) opened in May 1939, the first art-house cinema in Britain outside London.

The exterior, designed by prolific cinema architect James McKissack was influenced by the Dutch modernist Willem Marinus Dudok, who was in turn heavily influenced by Frank Lloyd Wright; this chain of reference is very apparent in the striking geometry of the building. The interior features curvilinear art deco detailing throughout, including in the doors, balconies, furniture and throughout the cafe-bar. The art deco style was popular in cinema design the world over and surviving examples of deco cinema facades in Glasgow include the Ascot in Anniesland (now converted into flats) and the Lyceum in Govan. It is rare, however, for these buildings to survive as functioning cinemas, and it is testament to the GFT's unique atmosphere and creative scheduling that it remains a popular film theatre, as originally intended.

The interior has changed considerably, however, since the '30s, to keep up with modern-day audience requirements. The foyer was originally double-height, with twin staircases leading to the balcony, but in 1968 it was reconfigured into a single-storey space, with a deco-style bar added on to the mezzanine.

In 1973, the Cosmo was bought by the Scottish Film Council, who undertook further changes, including subdividing the single 850-seat auditorium and also changing its name to its current title. The GFT has been visited over the years by many luminaries of the movie industry, including David Lynch, Martin Scorsese and Quentin Tarantino.

The cinema was originally advertised in the press as 'Entertainment for the Discriminating' and whether today's customers want to see *Battleship Potemkin* or a Hollywood extravaganza, GFT's interiors give an atmosphere steeped in history that its modern counterparts would find hard to match.

Galleries

Gallery of Modern Art

The imposing Gallery of Modern Art, known locally as GoMA, was originally built as a home for wealthy tobacco lord William Cunninghame in 1778 for the princely sum of £10,000. The surrounding area was still rural farmland on the western fringes of Glasgow and, when completed, this mansion was said to be one of the grandest townhouses in Scotland. In 1827, the mansion became Glasgow's new Royal Exchange, formerly situated at the Tontine Building on the Trongate.

Architect David Hamilton (see also Hutchesons' Hall, pp. 129–131, and the Corinthian, pp. 137–141) adapted the building for its new purposes, adding the main hall to the rear of the building, and the elaborate entrance portico and Corinthian columns to the front. For the next 100 years, the building was run as the Exchange, trading in tobacco, sugar, rum, molasses, coal and iron, becoming the heart of Glasgow's business community.

Following this period, further uses of the building included the city's first telephone exchange, a restaurant and the Stirling Library. In 1996, after 220 years of history and a £7.2 million makeover, it was transformed into the Gallery of Modern Art.

Date: 1778; later adaptation, 1827–30

Architect adaptation: David Hamilton

Address: Royal Exchange Square

Status: A-listed

Original purpose: residential

Opposite. The main gallery, with Jim Lambie's installation Forever Changes (part of Glasgow International 2008). Image courtesy of The Artist and The Modern Institute / Toby Webster Ltd, Glasgow, photograph: Keith Hunter

McLellan Galleries

Date: 1856; 1904; 1913–14

Architect: James Smith;
Frank Burnet and Boston;
A.B. Macdonald

Address:
254–270 Sauchiehall Street

Status: B-listed

Original purpose: gallery

*Opposite. The southern
reception areas of the gallery.*

The McLellan Galleries were built for the specific purpose of providing gallery space for the art collection of local businessman and patron of the arts Archibald McLellan. The McLellan family had made their fortune in the city through a successful coach-building firm, and Archibald was a keen collector and philanthropist; he was friends with many of the most prominent artists, writers and creatives of the day. His paintings collection, with a focus on old masters, was internationally significant and included works by Titian and Botticelli. When McLellan died, he intended to bequeath both his art collection and the galleries, which were then under construction, to the city; however, his considerable debts meant they had to be sold, and Glasgow Town Council eventually purchased the property and its collection for £44,500, believing the collection to be of major value to the city and intending the building to become Glasgow's main art gallery.

The building was designed by James Smith, partner of David Hamilton (Gallery of Modern Art, Hutchesons' Hall, the Corinthian), with whom he worked on Royal Exchange Square, amongst other prominent Glasgow buildings. Anecdotally, James was the father of infamous Glasgow socialite Madeleine Smith, who, in one of the most colourful incidents in the history of Glasgow's Victorian society, was accused of and tried for murdering her illicit French lover with arsenic. The trial took place the year after the McLellan was built. She was found not guilty, despite strong evidence against her: the verdict was discussed as being not least due to her influential architect father's societal position and contacts.

The most striking space within the Galleries is the Sauchiehall Street entrance hall, with its dramatic double staircase, marble Corinthian column-lined landing and ornate decorative plasterwork. The landing is top-lit by a beautiful cupola of Glasgow Style stained glass. The large gallery spaces are flooded with natural light from the skylights. The building housed the Glasgow School of Art from 1869 until 1899, when it moved into the Mackintosh-designed campus directly behind the

galleries. It retains an intrinsic link with the GSA and in the aftermath of the School's 2014 fire was used as vital decant space for artefacts rescued from the Renfrew Street building.

A major fire at the McLellan in the 1980s led to a £3 million restoration and it reopened in 1990 as one of the best-equipped high-specification galleries in the UK. In 1996, it played host to the Glasgow leg of a major international touring exhibition of the Mackintosh-designed Ingram Street Tearooms. Since then it has been used for a variety of successful exhibitions and events, and there is an ongoing campaign to secure this much-loved city-centre building a sustainable future.

Overleaf. The ceiling of the Sauchiehall Street entranceway features elaborate plasterwork and Glasgow Style glazing in the cupola.

Centre for Contemporary Arts

The renowned Alexander Thomson-designed Grecian Chambers on Sauchiehall Street is heavy with the exotic detailing and motifs 'Greek' Thomson is famous for (see 4 Great Western Terrace, pp. 17–21, for more on Thomson); the interiors within, along with a small grouping of buildings behind and around the chambers, have now been converted to Glasgow's Centre for Contemporary Arts (CCA).

Glasgow architectural practice Page\Park undertook a comprehensive conservation and redevelopment project of the building in the late 1990s, removing unsympathetic additions which had built up over the decades (or as the architects succinctly describe it, undertaking an exercise in 'archaeological undoing'), rediscovering a hidden villa within the building group and, most notably, covering the open central courtyard with a high-level glass roof. The light-flooded 'courtyard' now functions as the central hub of the complex and houses the cafe-bar, with a series of steel bridges, walkways and staircases connecting it with the arts spaces, cinema and offices within the surrounding buildings.

Well situated for the nearby Glasgow School of Art's students and faculty, it is a popular space in the city for contemporary art, art-house cinema, dining, drinking and general revelry.

Date: 1865 / 2001

Architect: Alexander Thomson; 2001 redevelopment, Page\Park architects

Address:
350 Sauchiehall Street

Status: A-listed

Original purpose:
commercial chambers

Opposite. The area now housing the popular cafe-bar was originally an open courtyard behind the Thomson-designed Grecian Chambers. Above is part of a surviving terrace pre-dating Thomson's building.

Overleaf. A recent redevelopment added a modern and industrial edge to the A-listed historic space, with the addition of steel walkways and the sleek glass roof.

Churches

Cottier's

The category A-listed Cottier Theatre, Bar and Restaurant was originally built as Dowanhill United Presbyterian Church by Glasgow architect William Leiper. Its architectural style is unique and was quite shocking when built; soon after its opening in the 1860s, the *Building News* declared of Leiper's design: 'The architect's aim has been to build a church which might have some claim to be reckoned "artistic".'

Leiper, best known in the city for the exotic Templeton's Carpet Factory at Glasgow Green, was fascinated with sculpture and included many sculptural features in his buildings, including a set of dogs' heads in the Gothic Revival exterior of the Dowanhill Church. Its distinctive steeple is visible from miles around; at a giant 195 feet, it is one of the best – and biggest – surviving in Glasgow.

The interior of the building is startlingly original. The designer was Daniel Cottier, stained-glass artist extraordinaire, entrepreneur and something of a Victorian equivalent to modern design gurus such as Terence Conran. After beginning his career in his native Glasgow with various commissions, including Dowanhill Church, Cottier moved to London to open his first shop, Cottier and Co., Art Furniture Makers, Glass and Tile Painters, where he had huge success in supplying fashionable

Date: 1865–6

Architect/designer: William Leiper, interior by Daniel Cottier

Address: 93–5 Hyndland Street

Status: A-listed

Original purpose: church

Opposite. The decorative scheme in the church is startlingly original in its bold use of colour and pattern. The south-east corner of the church displays the bold use of colour and pattern.

Above. The church is now a thriving theatre.

furnishings to the great and the good of Victorian London. In 1873, he branched out and started trading in New York, later also opening a studio in Australia. The Sydney branch went from strength to strength, becoming for a time the most famous and celebrated decorating firm in Australia.

Cottier had a profound effect on the city in terms of the holistic artist-designer, as historian Juliet Kinchin suggests: 'Arguably Dowanhill Church [Cottier's] is the most significant survivor of a number of projects in the 1860s that made a contribution to the development of the local skill base and stimulated the kind of adventurous patronage that paved the way for

the emergence of Glasgow as an international centre for progressive design around 1900. It provided a model for a new kind of "art" architecture involving a non-hierarchical collaboration between architect and decorative artist that embraced every aspect of the building, from the railings outside through to the collection plates within the interior.'

The following decades took their toll on Dowanhill Church, and by the 1980s it was in a semi-derelict condition. It was purchased from the Church of Scotland by the Four Acres Charitable Trust, a building preservation trust, for £1, with the ambition to restore the building and transform

Above. One of the restaurant spaces within the former Dowanhill Church.

it into a theatre and bar complex. The unique stained glass and decorative scheme led to the building bearing the name of the designer and Cottier's was born. Over the following years, the fabric of the building was secured and the halls were converted into the bar and restaurant. The sanctuary was successfully used as a theatre from 1994 until 2004, playing host to many theatrical and musical performances. Recent conservation work has reinstated the theatre, restoring its unique decoration. The organ has likewise been restored and the basement excavated to add modern facilities.

The Four Acres Charitable Trust have recently applied a similar

business model to Webster's on Great Western Road, formerly Landsdowne Parish Church, the dramatic Victorian Gothic building designed by famed local architect John Honeyman, also known in Glasgow for the Ca' D'Oro Building (and as a colleague of Charles Rennie Mackintosh). This church also has remarkable windows. In 1913, local stained-glass artist, GSA alumnus and one of Glasgow's great pioneers of stained-glass art, Alf Webster was commissioned to design two new memorial windows. His designs show a variety of scenes from the Bible in a highly stylised and strikingly modern form.

Structures

Argyll Arcade

Argyll Arcade is one of Europe's oldest covered shopping arcades, and the first of its kind in Scotland. Designed in 1827 by the eminent Scottish architect John Baird (also famous for the grand Gardner's Warehouse on Jamaica Street and what is now Princes Square shopping mall on Buchanan Street), the arcade was not only the first but is now the last remaining of its type in the country. One hundred years ago, all Scotland's cities had an arcade; in Glasgow, there were several. As the only one left, Argyll Arcade is truly unique and a signifier of the city's successful retail heritage.

With more than thirty jewellers, the Argyll Arcade has the largest selection of diamond jewellery in a single location in Scotland. One of the jewellers, Mr Harold and Sons, has been called 'Glasgow's answer to Tiffany's', the famous New York store, due to the remarkable array of diamonds in the window displays. Samuel Groundland, manager and the 'Son' from the shop's name, has worked in the arcade for thirty years: 'It makes a difference to be within the arcade, which over the years has definitely become the "Jewellery Quarter" of the city,' he says. 'We are a family business, and we have customers who have had previous generations of their own families buy special pieces from us over the years

Date: 1827

Architect: John Baird

Address:
Buchanan Street–Argyle Street

Status: A-listed

Original purpose:
shopping arcade

Opposite. Argyll Arcade is one of Europe's oldest covered shopping arcades.

Right. The elegant covered arcade is reminiscent of those found in Paris and Brussels and is a great reminder of Glasgow's tradition as a retail centre.

Opposite. Above shop level sits a floor of traditional workshops and offices, some of them jeweller's workshops servicing the retail spaces below.

'...I think the historic architecture of the arcade definitely emphasises that sense of nostalgia and heritage involved in buying jewellery.'

Glasgow has built successfully on its strong retail heritage and Buchanan Street, just to the west of the arcade, remains the busiest shopping thoroughfare in the UK after Oxford Street in London.

The Kibble Palace

Date: 1863–6

Architect/engineer:
John Kibble

Address: Botanic Gardens

Status: A-listed

Original purpose: glasshouse

Whether to marvel at the Victorian ironwork, study the world-renowned collection of exotic plants or warm up in the Mediterranean conditions, the Kibble Palace in Glasgow's Botanic Gardens is one of the most popular and picturesque spots in the city.

The 2,137-metre square iron-and-glass structure was originally designed in the 1860s by John Kibble, a Scottish inventor and engineer, as a conservatory for his home on Loch Long. The ironwork was produced by Walter Macfarlane's world-famous Saracen Foundry in Possil (see 22 Park Circus, pp. 23–27). In 1871, Kibble offered the grand structure to the Glasgow Corporation for re-erection in Queen's Park, but they failed to take up the offer immediately and he instead offered it to the Royal Botanic Institution of Glasgow. They promptly accepted, and the glasshouse was erected in the Botanic Gardens the following year after being sailed 'doon the water' from Loch Long.

The duly-named Kibble Palace became home to a wide variety of plants which botanists travelled all over the world to collect, including a collection of Australian tree ferns, some of which have now lived there for more than 120 years.

As well as its notable plants, the Palace has attracted international praise for its dramatic curvilinear architecture, with the *Architects' Journal* of 6 May 1964 stating: 'The Kibble Palace is one of the most astonishing buildings in Glasgow . . . enclosed by a marvellous glass dome, light as a spider's web.'

Throughout its history, the Kibble Palace has been host to many diverse events, from rectorial inaugurations in the 1870s and public concerts (including somewhat surprisingly a 1980s Barry Manilow extravaganza) to Shakespearean plays and fashion shows in more recent times.

Not least because of the climate, Glasgow has a strong tradition of Victorian winter gardens; while the Kibble Palace is perhaps the most celebrated, other notable examples can be found at Tollcross Park, Springburn Park, Queen's Park (where parrots used to flutter amongst the

foliage) and the People's Palace at Glasgow Green.

Between 2003 and 2006, the Kibble Palace underwent a £7 million conservation programme, involving its complete dismantling and the removal of the parts for conservation work to Yorkshire. This was the first time in the Kibble's 130-year history in Glasgow that the plant collection was completely removed from the Palace, until it reopened to the public once again in winter 2006.

Opposite. The cast ironwork for the Kibble was produced by Walter Macfarlane's world-famous Saracen Foundry.

Left. Detail of the intricate cast iron finials and brackets.

The Briggait

The Briggait houses what has been referred to as 'Scotland's most important collection of surviving market halls'. Originally built in the nineteenth century as a home for the city's fish market, it has played a key role in the social and cultural history of the city. However, following the relocation of the fish traders and a tumultuous history, it languished empty for more than twenty years until its recent reincarnation as artists' studios and a creative industries space.

The building was inspired by Les Halles, the great market in Paris, built between 1845 and 1854, and the French Renaissance style is prevalent throughout the exterior and elegant interior.

The interior structure of the Briggait encompasses the seventeenth-century Merchants' Steeple and is formed of a central, balconied main hall and two smaller halls, topped with a magnificent cast-iron and glass roof. The central hall was the original trading room for Glasgow's wholesale fish trade and was designed to allow horse-drawn carts to enter, load and unload their wares. The walls were built with glazed white bricks, popular in Victorian markets for their hygienic qualities.

When the fish market moved to an out-of-town site in the late 1970s, the building became redundant and the council moved to demolish it. A trust was formed to save the building, and funds were raised to repair it and convert it into a shopping atrium, with food and craft stalls. In 2011, a £6.3 million redevelopment project saw the space transformed into the cultural industries hub it is today, with the creation of seventy workspaces for artists and cultural tenants; retail and exhibition space; a cafe; and future plans to implement facilities for circus, dance, physical theatre, street arts, trapeze and aerial performance.

The redevelopment has provided an important new space for artists and creative industries professionals, and it has contributed to the ongoing regeneration of the Merchant City area.

Date: 1873 / 1886 / 1903

Architect: Clarke and Bell

Address: 141 Bridgegate

Status: A-listed

Original purpose: fish market

Opposite. The original building was extended in 1886 and again in 1903 to incorporate a seventeenth-century steeple, which now protrudes through the roof.
(Photograph: Andrew Lee)

Overleaf. The central hall.
(Photograph: Andrew Lee)

Cafes, Bars, Restaurants

Hutchesons' Hall

Hutchesons' Hall on Ingram Street in the heart of Glasgow's Merchant City has been used in recent years as a shop, gallery and events space, under the National Trust for Scotland's ownership. Environmental damage in early 2008 rendered it unsuitable for public access; however, since then, a full redevelopment, including essential repair works, has recently transformed this magnificent building and brought it back to life as the bar and restaurant Hutchesons'.

The hall was built to replace the former seventeenth-century Hutchesons' Hospital on the Trongate, which was demolished in the late eighteenth century as part of a wider programme of redevelopment in the area. The hospital was founded by George and Thomas Hutcheson, wealthy Glasgow lawyers, landowners and philanthropists, who bequeathed a sum of money for the construction of a hospital for poor craftsmen and 'the decrepit old men of Glasgow', to take care of them in their final days. (The brothers also funded Hutchesons' Grammar School, now in the south of the city, originally built as a school for orphans.)

Following the demise of the original hospital, the Ingram Street building was designed in 1802 by local architectural hero David Hamilton (perhaps most famous in Glasgow for the Royal Exchange; see Gallery of

Date: 1802–5

Architect: David Hamilton; 1876 refurbishment, John Baird

Address: Ingram Street

Status: A-listed

Original purpose: hospital

Opposite. One of the stunning original tiled fireplaces in the upstairs hall; the interior of the A-listed building was remodelled in 1876, adding lavish stained glass, wooden panelling and detailed plasterwork.

Modern Art, p. 99). Two sculptures, depicting the Hutcheson brothers, were saved from the seventeenth-century hospital and now take pride of place, integrated into the building's facade. They are widely believed to be the oldest portrait sculptures in the city.

While little has changed on the outside of the building (aside from the sandstone having been painted), the interior was remodelled in 1876 by Hamilton's former pupil, fellow Glaswegian John Baird II (one-time partner of Alexander 'Greek' Thomson). This reconstruction of the inside of the building created the dramatic double-height hall, with lavish stained glass, wooden panelling and detailed plasterwork, that can still be seen there today.

A recent phase of repairs and its transformation into a bar and restaurant has safeguarded the building for future generations by giving it contemporary purpose; allowing the legacy of the Hutcheson brothers, as well as the design genius of Hamilton and Baird, to endure.

Sloans Cafe Bar

Date: 1827–8; remodelled, 1900

Architect: original building, John Baird; 1900 adaptation, Charles H. Robinson

Address: 62 Argyll Arcade

Status: A-listed

Original purpose: cafe

Opposite. Glasgow Style stained glass amidst the typical Victorian interior at Sloans Cafe Bar.

Overleaf. Turn-of-the-century Glasgow Style tiling in the entrance foyer of Sloans.

Hidden away just off the main shopping streets of the city sits Sloans cafe bar, claimed to be the oldest public bar in Glasgow, dating back to the early 1800s. At the south end of the atmospheric Argyll Arcade (see pp. 115–116), it has been providing refreshments to customers since the arcade opened, originally as the Arcade Cafe, becoming David Sloan's Arcade Cafe at the turn of the twentieth century. It was at this time that a major redevelopment took place, incorporating the addition of a beautiful array of Glasgow Style stained glass and tiling amidst the typical Victorian fittings, combining to make a striking, unique and wholly modern interior. The ballroom in particular is a highly evocative space, and surviving architectural elements such as the original small kiosk on the half-landing add further to the high-Victorian atmosphere.

The tiled entrance from Argyll Arcade is a stunning example of the city's turn-of-the-century embrace of exotic, highly stylised tiling and the high quality timberwork, including the arcaded glazed screens and dramatic staircase, are notable features. Charles Robinson, the designer responsible for the redevelopment, specialised in ornate bar interiors and very few examples of his work are thought to survive. Unusually, the listing status of Sloans was upgraded from category B to A in 1996, in recognition of the significance and rarity of the art nouveau/Glasgow Style cafe interior.

Sloans' location in Argyll Arcade, a centre for the purchase of 'occasion' jewellery, adds to the bar's unique environment: 'Traditionally, couples came to the arcade to buy engagement and wedding rings and would then head to Sloans to celebrate,' comments Kimberley Gallagher, the bar's events manager. 'We love being part of that and it definitely adds an element of excitement and romance to the bar. Not many places in Glasgow have such history and character as we do here in the Arcade.'

The Corinthian

When talking to locals about Glasgow's historic interiors with 'wow' factor, often the first building mentioned is the Corinthian. It encapsulates everything the Glasgow interior should offer: grandeur, scale, elaborate detailing, including a jaw-dropping 26-foot ceiling dome, combined with a hefty dose of modern glamour.

The former bank stands on the site of the Virginia Mansion, constructed for prominent city merchant George Buchanan and famed as being one of the finest private residences in Glasgow (similar to the nearby Gallery of Modern Art, p. 99).

The original home was knocked down and architect David Hamilton (see also Hutchesons' Hall, pp. 129–130, and the Gallery of Modern Art) was employed to build the Glasgow and Ship Bank, later to become the Union Bank of Scotland.

The building was, and still is, one of the most elaborate in Glasgow; however, in 1920 the building was converted into courts and the redevelopment hid many of the original historic features. In 1999, the city's G1 entertainment group bought the building and restored it, reinstating such details as the Doric pilastrade, cornicing, cupola, plasterwork and sculptures, which almost unbelievably had been concealed for nearly eighty years.

A further interior redevelopment phase in 2010, which incorporated a casino into the property, amongst other changes, upheld the Corinthian's tradition of using acclaimed local architects, artists and artisans by engaging world-renowned interior designers Graven Images.

Date: 1841–2

Architect: David Hamilton; later adaptations, James Salmon Snr, John Burnet

Address: 191 Ingram Street

Status: A-listed

Original purpose: bank

Opposite. The Corinthian is one of the most striking interiors in the city. (Photograph: Renzo Mazzolini)

Right. The ground floor Bootleg Bar incorporates traditional bank safes into its design, while the floor features a 500,000-piece mosaic depicting Queen Victoria as she appeared on old banknotes – a nod to the building's past life as the Union Bank of Scotland. (Photograph: Renzo Mazzolini)

Opposite. The 26-foot dome is the centrepiece of the ground-floor bar. (Photograph: Renzo Mazzolini)

Left. The opulent hallway integrates original features such as the beautiful mosaic tiled floor, elaborate staircase and ornate cornicing, with contemporary additions of mirrors and dramatic lighting to create an undeniable 'wow' factor. (Photograph: Renzo Mazzolini)

Right. This lavish former bank now features a casino. (Photograph: Renzo Mazzolini)

De Quincey House/Cup Tea Lounge

Date: 1888–9

Architect: Alfred Waterhouse

Address: 71 Renfield Street

Status: B-listed

Original purpose: commercial offices

Opposite. The old 'telling room' of this former insurance office features exotic tiles, an elaborately decorated ceiling and elegant archways.

Overleaf. The dramatic tiled ceiling.

De Quincey House acquires its name from Thomas De Quincey, the famous English writer. Best known for his reckless lifestyle and as the author of *Confessions of an English Opium Eater,* he lived in Glasgow for a short time while hiding from his creditors. The Victorian Gothic building was designed by Alfred Waterhouse of Natural History Museum fame and the glorious tiles abundantly used throughout are from Burmantofts, one of the premier tile manufacturers in Europe of the period, based in Leeds (see also City Chambers, pp. 77–83).

Originally built as the offices of the Prudential Insurance Co., the venue has hosted a range of catering establishments over the past decades with varying levels of debauchery, although current occupiers Cup Tea Lounge err on the more genteel side of refreshments than some of their predecessors.

Tearooms in Glasgow have an illustrious history, wrapped up with the social context of the city. The temperance movement was strongly embraced in Glasgow as an antidote to widespread problems of alcoholism, and many tearooms sprang up to provide citizens with the 'cup that cheers but does not inebriate'. The first tearoom in the UK was, in fact, set up in Glasgow in 1875, courtesy of local tea dealer Stuart Cranston, whose sister Kate went on to achieve fame in the city for her chain of 'artistic' tearooms. For these, she employed the most progressive and avant-garde local artists and artisans, such as George Walton, Charles Rennie Mackintosh and Margaret MacDonald, to design the interiors and, for the first time, specifically targeted urban women as customers.

Similar to that of Sloans Cafe Bar (see pp. 132–135), Cup Tea Lounge has a striking Glasgow Style entrance vestibule, featuring beautiful faience tiles. The tiles continue throughout the interior, including, unusually, on the ceiling.

Right. The interior is brought to life with the shiny and colourful faience tiles that decorate the walls, pillars and entrance vestibule.

Opposite. The tiles used throughout are from the Leeds-based manufacturer Burmantofts.

University Cafe

Date: c.1918

Architect: unknown

Address: 87 Byres Road

Status: unlisted

Original purpose: cafe

Opposite. The woodwork in the interior was crafted by the original owner-proprietor, an Italian carpenter who came to Glasgow to work in the shipyards.

Overleaf. Art deco features include the striking wall clock.

Pages 152–153. An archive photo of the cafe taken soon after it opened in 1918 hangs in pride of place on the wall, showing the current owner-manager Carlo's grandparents, who established it.

The University Cafe is a Byres Road institution, popular with families, students and locals for its traditional food, friendly service and made-on-the-premises ice cream. While not listed, the interior is important in terms of Glasgow's social and design history, and is perhaps one of the best surviving examples of the Glasgow phenomenon of early twentieth-century traditional Italian family-run cafes.

Glasgow has a strong Italian community; many migrants moved to the city in the late nineteenth century to escape economic hardship and famine in Italy, hoping to make a new life in Scotland. Many worked in the restaurant business: in fact, it is estimated that there were over 300 Italian-run catering establishments in Glasgow by 1905. The current owner of the University Cafe, Carlo Verrecchia, has been running the cafe for more than forty years. His grandfather came to Glasgow from Cassino in southern Italy in the early 1900s to work as a carpenter in the city's thriving shipyards. He soon made enough money to set up a traditional Italian cafe and in 1918 the University Cafe was born. As a trained carpenter, he did all the woodwork for the interior himself and the fine workmanship, which still looks superb nearly 100 years on, is a testament to his skills and the quality of the traditional rosewood used. The cafe has since been passed down to Carlo.

The interior, while typical of British interwar-period design, has several art deco touches, including the stylized wall clock, streamline moderne front door and much-loved window displays.

Other authentic examples in the city of Italian-Glaswegian family-run cafes that have survived to become local institutions include Fazzi in Garnethill and Cafe D'Jaconelli in Maryhill.

UNIVERSITY CAFE

PASTAS | PASTAS

Streets: Byres Road By Night   Jim Simpson

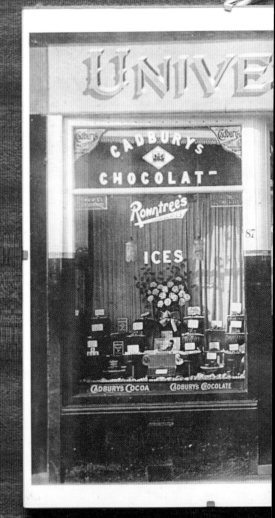

UNIVE

CADBURYS
CHOCOLAT

Rowntree's

87

ICES

CADBURYS COCOA   CADBURYS CHOCOLATE

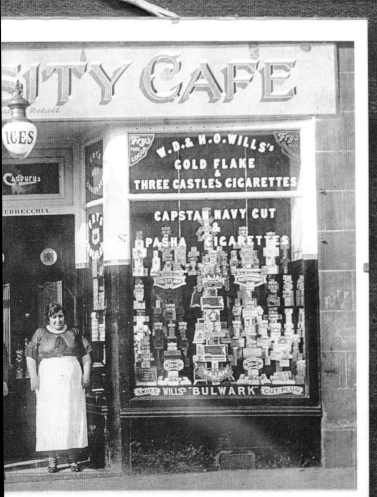

Rogano

Convivial, glamorous and nostalgic are words often used to describe the Rogano, one of the city's most atmospheric restaurants and a local institution. Originally established as a Victorian sherry bodega in the late nineteenth century, in 1936 the building was taken over by Don Grant, who, having just returned from the maiden voyage of the Clyde-built *Queen Mary* ocean liner, decorated the Rogano in the same nautical-inspired style. Glass panels in the downstairs restaurant decorated with etched octopuses and other creatures from the deep add to the seafaring ambience; these panels were rescued from the swimming pool area of the *Queen Mary* herself.

The Rogano is one of the most well-known examples in Glasgow of an original art deco interior design. The art deco movement, emerging out of Continental Europe in the 1920s, epitomised an age of jazz, glamour and decadence, and was for a period the design choice *du jour* for commercial ventures such as restaurants.

As architectural historian and art deco specialist Charles MacKean has commented: 'In a city like Glasgow, art deco buildings shook up the architecture of industrial Scotland. Suddenly, you had these sleek buildings that were shiny, or brilliant white, or with dazzling chrome fascias, appearing in soot black streets . . . They were buildings designed to draw people in, and get them to open their wallets. They symbolised the start of the consumer age.'

Over the years, the Rogano has been visited by the stars of stage and screen, including Liberace, Joan Collins and Elizabeth Taylor. Today, it maintains its unique intimate ambience and old-world glamour, which has lured in the celebrities and kept the locals coming back over the years. Ann Patterson, the general manager, says, 'There is so much history to the Rogano and we have a large proportion of regulars. When you become part of people's lives and a family's traditions, it creates a rare and intimate atmosphere and we are very proud of that.'

Date: 1935–6

Architect/designer:
John Thompson; 1935 refurbishment,
Charles Cameron Baillie

Address: 11 Exchange Place

Status: B-listed

Original purpose: restaurant

Opposite. The upstairs cafe area.

Opposite. The Art Deco booths in the bar area.

Left. Contemporary art deco-style glass in the downstairs restaurant.

Overleaf. The upstairs bar area, showing the iconic streamline booths, sleek deco mirrors and nautical wall motifs, referencing Glasgow's shipbuilding heritage.

Select Bibliography

Baudelaire, Charles 'On the Heroism of Modern Life' in *The Salon of 1846*
(Oxford University Press, 1975)

Blazwick, Iwona Ed *Century City: Art and Culture in the Modern Metropolis*
(Tate Publishing, 2001)

*Cottier's in Context: Daniel Cottier, William Leiper and Dowanhill Church,
Glasgow, Case Study 3* (Historic Scotland, 2014)

Foreman, Carol *Hidden Glasgow* (Birlinn, 2001)

Friedman, Joe *Inside London – Discovering the Classic Interiors of London*
(Phaidon, 1988)

Glendinning, Miles, Ranald MacInnes and Aonghus MacKechnie *A History
of Scottish Architecture* (Edinburgh University Press, 1996)

Gomme, Andor Harvey and David Walker *Architecture of Glasgow* (Lund
Humphries Publishers/John Smith & Sons, London, 1987)

Gow, Ian *The Scottish Interior: Georgian and Victorian Architecture*
(Edinburgh University Press, 1992)

Greenhalgh, Paul *Art Nouveau 1890–1914* (V&A, 2000)

Jacobs, Jane *The Death and Life of Great American Cities* (Vintage, 1993)

Kinchin, Perilla *Tea and Taste: The Glasgow Tea Rooms, 1875–1975* (White
Cockade Publishing, 1991)

McKean, Charles *The Scottish Thirties – An Architectural Introduction*
(Edinburgh, 1987)

Urquhart, Gordon *Along Great Western Road: An Illustrated History of
Glasgow's West End* (Stenlake Publishing, 2000)

Acknowledgements

We would like to thank for their help, advice, access and support throughout this project: Jemma Allan, Gordon Barr, Fraser & Siobhan at Albany, all at Birlinn, Judith Bowers, Nancy Braid, Fabiane Cabral, Ken & Margaret Cairnduff, Pat Cassidy, Karin Currie, Liz Davidson, Robert Gibbs, Glasgow City Heritage Trust, Diane Goudie, Ruth Johnson, Alex Kapranos, Stefan King, Ann Laing, Jim Lambie, Kirsty Lang, Andrew Lee, Ranald MacInnes, Tom Manley, Renzo Mazzolini, Hugh McCafferty, Aasma Mohammad, Herve Moulin, Ann Patterson, David Robertson, James Rusk, Chris Trainer, Gordon Urquhart, Carlo Verrecchia, Sarah Watt.

The author produced a series of articles for *i-on* magazine from 2008 to 2011 under the title 'Iconic Glasgow', exploring historic buildings in the city. Some of the material produced for this series appears here in revised form and we thank *i-on* magazine's editor Susie Cormack and publisher, Treacle Productions, for their support.

We also thank those not mentioned above who have with generosity and trust let us into their fabulous properties.

Finally, thanks to Sergei for enduring some long, sometimes dusty shoots with great humour and keeping us entertained.